DRIVING SKILLS

YOUR DRIVING TEST

London: HMSO

Originated by The Driving Standards Agency

Prepared by COMIND

Developed and Designed by Nick Lynch

Graphics by Vicky Squires and Stephen Oakman

Published by HMSO

ISBN 0 11 551158 X

*Other titles in the
Driving Skills series*

The Motorcycling Manual
ISBN 0 11 550974 7

The Driving Manual
ISBN 0 11 551054 0

*Your Large Goods Vehicle
Driving Test*
ISBN 0 11 551192 X

"Safe Driving for Life"

This book is aimed at those who are currently learning – or who are about to learn – to drive a car or ride a motorcycle.

There are many myths about driving, riding motorcycles, and even more about the driving test. We hope to dispel these by giving you sound advice on what you need to learn and how driving tests are conducted.

The Driving Standards Agency (DSA) is an Executive Agency of the Department of Transport.

We are responsible for all driving tests, supervising the instruction given by ADIs (instructors approved to give car driving lessons) and the private organisations involved in motorcycle compulsory basic training.

We are the authoritive body for all matters relating to driving and riding techniques.

Each year nearly one million people decide they want to learn either to drive a car or to ride a moped or motorcycle. You and most of the others will go on to take a driving test.

The purpose of the driving test is to see if you can drive your vehicle safely on the road. It is vitally important to develop the right attitude towards driving, and to drive at all times with responsibility and consideration for those who are sharing the road with you.

Only those who can do this earn the right to drive a vehicle without supervision, without L-plates, and on motorways.

The test is just one stage in your driving or riding career. You should not assume that if you pass the test, you are a good driver or rider with nothing more to learn. The instruction you receive before the test is the foundation for gaining knowledge, skills and experience.

Your driving career started the moment you decided that you wanted to be able to drive a car or ride a motorcycle on the road. The fact that you are now reading this book confirms that you have made a good start. Make sure that your aim is at all times, *safe driving for life.*

David E Norris
Chief Driving Examiner
Driving Standards Agency

Contents

Continued ☞

Contents (cont'd)

See for yourself what the test is *really* like.

**YOUR DRIVING TEST –
The Video** complements
this book and explodes
many myths by showing
that the test is not as bad as
you think.

Lasting approximately one
hour, the video is available
from HMSO Bookshops,
HMSO direct, major
bookshops and all good
video retailers.

This book will help you to

- Learn to drive competently
- Prepare for and pass your driving test

Section 1 tells you what you need to do before the test.

Section 2 gives the test requirements and sound advice, simply and clearly. Refer to it regularly while you are learning and use it to check your progress.

If you are a learner moped rider or motorcyclist, Section 3 will tell you all you need to know about Compulsory Basic Training (CBT) and the motorcycle test.

Section 4 contains the official syllabus for learning to drive and lists the skills you need to master before taking your test. Refer to it regularly.

The important factors

This book is one of the important factors in your training: the others are

- A good instructor (see page 4)
- Plenty of practice
- Your attitude

You must manage your own learning.

Aim to be a competent and safe driver or motorcyclist, and not just to pass the test.

Driving is a life skill.

Your driving test is only the first step.

Motorcyclists

Study the Driving Standards Agency's book, *The Motorcycling Manual* (HMSO).

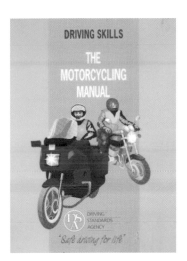

Further essential reading for all drivers

The Driving Standards Agency's publication, *The Driving Manual* (HMSO), sets out sound, safe and well-tried driving methods.

It's the Approved Driving Instructor's principal reference book.

You can buy it from any good bookshop.

The driving test is straightforward

You will pass if

You can show the examiner that you can

- Drive safely
- Do the set exercises
- Show a thorough know-ledge of The Highway Code

Does the standard of the test vary?

No! All examiners are trained to carry out tests to the same standard.

Test routes

- Are as uniform as possible
- Include a range of typical road and traffic conditions

You should have the same result from different examiners or at different Driving Test Centres.

Are examiners supervised?

Yes! They are closely supervised. A senior officer may sit in on your test.

Don't worry about this.

The senior officer won't be examining you, but making sure the examiner is testing you properly.

Since the senior officer will not interfere with the test or the result, just carry on as if he or she wasn't there.

Can anyone else accompany you on the test?

Yes! Your instructor is allowed to be present during the test but must not take any part in it.

You should bring an interpreter with you, if you need one, but you are not allowed to use your instructor for that purpose.

Can you use a car which is 'automatic' for the test?

Yes! When you pass your test, your full driving licence will entitle you to drive an 'automatic' car.

It will also act as a provisional licence for a car with a manual gearbox.

What will the examiner want from you?

The examiner will want to see you drive safely and competently under various road and traffic conditions.

He (or she) will

- Give you directions clearly and in good time
- Ask you to carry out set exercises

The examiner will be understanding and sympathetic, and will make every effort to put you at ease.

However, to avoid distracting you, the examiner will say as little as possible while you're driving.

How should you drive during the test?

Drive in the way your instructor has taught you.

If you make a mistake, don't worry. It might be minor and may not affect your result.

The examiner will be looking for an overall safe standard and you will not fail for one minor mistake.

How long will the test last?

About 35 minutes.

Note: The extended test for persons convicted of serious motoring offences will last approximately twice as long (see Section 5)

 What will the test include?

Apart from general driving which we will talk about later, your test will include

- An eyesight test (if you fail this, the test will not go any further)
- Special exercises, such as an emergency stop, and two of the following
  - reversing round a corner
  - turning in the road
  - reverse parking
- Questions on
  - The Highway Code
  - other motoring matters

(The questions are usually asked at the end of the driving test.)

 What about the special exercises?

The special exercises will take place at carefully selected places on the test route.

The examiner will be as helpful as possible, and for each exercise will

- Ask you to pull up at the left side of the road
- Explain the exercise and ask you to carry it out

Make sure you understand!

Listen carefully to the explanation, but if you're not sure about anything, ask! The examiner will explain again.

 What's the purpose of the test?

The driving test is designed to see if

- You can drive safely
- You know and understand The Highway Code
- You understand other motoring matters, such as
  - what causes skids and how to control them
  - the importance of car maintenance

The test ensures that all drivers reach a minimum standard.

When you have passed

You'll be allowed to drive

- Without L-plates
- Unsupervised
- On motorways

However, it takes lots of practice to become a really skilled driver. Further tuition and the *Pass Plus* scheme are strongly recommended.

Your Provisional Driving Licence

You must hold a valid signed Provisional Driving Licence before you attempt to drive on the road.

Ask for the application form D1 at your local Post Office.

Why you should use an Approved Driving Instructor (ADI)

An Approved Driving Instructor is approved by the Driving Standards Agency to teach learner drivers for payment.

The Driving Standards Agency is responsible for maintaining and checking the standards for all ADIs.

You must use an ADI or trainee licence holder

If you want to learn to drive and pay someone to teach you.

It is unlikely that anyone except an ADI will have the experience, knowledge and training to teach you properly.

ADIs must

- Have held a full driving licence for four years
- Pass a difficult 3-part examination
- Reach and keep up a high standard of instruction
- Be registered with the Driving Standards Agency
- Display an ADI identification certificate on the windscreen of the tuition vehicle

Friends and relatives

If you are taking lessons with an ADI, it's a good idea to take extra practice with a friend or relative.

Ask your ADI for advice on this.

Take advice from your ADI on

- All aspects of driving
- What books to read
- When you will be ready for the test
- How to practise

How to choose an ADI

- Ask friends and relatives
- Choose an instructor
  - who has a good reputation
  - is reliable and punctual
  - whose car suits you

Note

Some trainee instructors are granted a trainee licence so they can gain teaching experience before their qualifying examination.

This is a pink identification certificate which must be displayed on the wind-screen of the tuition vehicle.

When you practise ...

You must have with you a person who

- Has held a full driving licence for at least three years and still holds one for the category of vehicle being driven
- Is at least 21 years of age

Vehicle insurance

The vehicle you practise in must be properly insured for you to drive. You will be asked to sign a declaration before the test begins.

If you drive while uninsured, you will be committing a serious offence.

Don't risk it!

How and where to practise

Practise

- On as many different types of road as you can
- In all sorts of traffic conditions — even in the dark

Practise

- The exercises included in the test, but don't concentrate solely on them

Practise

- On dual carriageways where the upper speed limit applies

You may be asked to drive on such roads during the test.

When you practise, try not to

- Obstruct traffic. Most drivers are tolerant of learners, but don't try their patience too much
- Annoy local residents. For example, by practising emergency stops in quiet, residential streets, or by practising on test routes
- Get in the way of someone taking a driving test. Try to be considerate

The Highway Code

You must

- Know and understand The Highway Code
- Obey it when driving
- Answer questions on it

So study it carefully!

When you are ready for the test

When will you be ready for the test?

When you can show that you have reached the standard set in this book.

Not before!

Ensure that all aspects of the official syllabus for learning to drive have been fully covered (see Section 4).

The learners who pass first time are the ones who are well instructed and get in plenty of practice.

They pass because **they wait until they're ready.**

How will you know when you're ready?

Your instructor will tell you. He (or she) has the knowledge and experience.

You must be able to drive

- *Consistently* well and with confidence
- Without assistance and guidance from your instructor

If you can't, you aren't ready for the test.

Most people who fail do so because they haven't had enough instruction and practice

They waste their money and the examiner's time.

Special circumstances

To make sure that enough time is allowed for your test, it would help the DSA to know

- If you are deaf or have severe hearing difficulties
- If you are restricted in any way in your movements
- If you have any disability which may affect your driving

So, if any of these applies to you, please write this on your application form.

If you can't speak English or are deaf, you are allowed to bring an interpreter who must not be your instructor.

Drivers with Disabilities

No matter how serious your disability might be, you will still take the same driving test as every other candidate.

However, more time is allowed for the test. This is simply so that your examiner can talk to you about your disability and any adaptations fitted to your vehicle.

For this reason, it is important to give details of your disability when you apply for your test.

If you would like further information, please see the list of useful addresses at the back of this book.

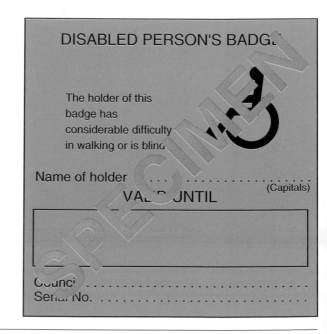

Driving Standards Agency

The application form

- You can obtain Form DL26 at any Driving Standards Agency Regional Office or Driving Test Centre.

  Your ADI will also be able to give you a copy and tell you the fee to send with it.

  Full details of all fees can be obtained from DSA Regional Offices or from your nearest Driving Test Centre.

- Complete the form, and send it with the appropriate fee to your Driving Standards Agency Regional Office.

- At test centres in Wales, you may wish to take the test in the Welsh language. Please indicate your choice on the application form.

- Apply well before the time you want to be tested.

- Give your preferred date.

Saturday and evening tests

Saturday and weekday evening tests are available at some driving test centres.

The fees for both are higher than for a test during normal working hours on weekdays.

Evening tests are available during the summer months only.

You can get details from

- DSA Regional Offices
- Driving Test Centres
- Your ADI

Driving Test Fees

You may pay by

- Cheque
- Postal order
- Credit card

Do not send cash

Full details are given on your application form.

Information on how to apply by using the Credit Card Hotline is given overleaf.

Your test appointment

Your DSA Regional Office will send you notification of your appointment, which is a receipt for your fee. Take it with you when you go for your test.

This will include

- The time and date of your appointment
- The address of the Driving Test Centre
- Other important information

If you have not received notification after two weeks, contact the DSA Regional Office straight away.

Postponing your test appointment

Contact your DSA Regional Office where you booked your test if

- The date or time of the appointment is not suitable
- You want to postpone or cancel the test

You must give at least 10 clear working days notice, (that is, two weeks—longer if there is a bank holiday) not counting

- The day the Office received your request
- The day of the test

If you don't give enough notice, you will lose your fee.

Booking by Credit or Debit Card Hotline

Visa, Mastercard, Switch and Delta.

You must be the card holder. If you are not, then the card holder must be present when a booking is made on the telephone.

The Credit Card "Hotline" telephone number for your area is shown on the application form and in the list of DSA Regional Offices given inside the back cover of this book.

If you use this service, the driving test booking clerk will be able to offer you an appointment over the telephone.

You should receive notification confirming the appointment within a few days.

When you telephone, make sure you have your completed application form with you.

The booking clerk will want the following details

- Your Driver Number shown on your licence
- The type of test you wish to book (eg. car or motorcycle)
- Your personal details (title, name, address, day/evening telephone contact numbers)
- Driving School Code No. (if known)
- Your preferred date
- Unacceptable days or periods
- If you can accept a short notice test (consult your ADI beforehand, if necessary)
- Disability or any special circumstance details
- Your Credit Card details (including Expiry Date)
- The Card Issue number when using SWITCH

Your driving licence

Make sure that you have
your provisional driving
licence with you, and that
you have signed it.

If you don't, you'll need
some other form of identity.
Any of the following is
acceptable

- A signed driving licence
  issued in

  - Great Britain,
    Northern Ireland,
    the Channel Islands,
    or the Isle of Man

  - an EC member state

  - a country whose
    driving licences can
    be exchanged for a
    United Kingdom
    Driving Licence

- A signed passport

- A signed International
  Driving Permit

- A signed British Forces
  Licence

- A signed identity card
  issued by your
  employer. This must
  show

  - your name written in
    roman letters (such
    as ordinary printing)

  - your photograph

The examiner might not be
able to conduct your test if
you cannot produce one of
these documents.

Remember, it's up to you to
satisfy the examiner of your
identity.

Your test vehicle

Make sure that the vehicle
you intend to drive or the
motorcycle you intend to
ride during your test is

- Legally roadworthy and
  has a current test
  certificate, if it is over
  the prescribed age

- Fully covered by
  insurance for its present
  use and for you to drive
  – especially if the vehicle
  is owned by a car-hire
  company. The examiner
  will ask you to sign a
  Declaration that your
  insurance is in order.
  The test will not be
  conducted if you are
  unable to do so

- Properly licensed with a
  valid tax disc displayed

- Displaying L-plates
  where required, which
  are visible from the front
  and rear

Both you and your
examiner must have a clear
view through the rear
window.

If you overlook any of these

- Your test may be
  cancelled

- You could lose your fee

For details of the moped and motorcycle test, please turn to Section 3

What the test requires

You must satisfy the examiner that, in good daylight, you can read a vehicle number-plate with letters 79.4mm (3.1 inches) high

Minimum distance

- 20.5 metres (about 67 feet), or
- 12.3 metres (about 40 feet) if you are operating a pedestrian-controlled vehicle.

If you need glasses

or contact lenses, wear them.

Continue to wear them during the test and whenever you drive or ride.

How the examiner will test you

Before you get into your car, the examiner will point out a vehicle and ask you to read the number-plate.

If you are unable to read the number-plate, the examiner will measure the exact distance and repeat the test.

If you fail the eyesight test

If you can't show the examiner that your eyesight is up to the standard required

- You will have failed your driving test
- Your test will go no further

If you normally wear glasses or contact lenses, wear them always when you drive or ride.

The Highway Code

You must

- Show knowledge and understanding of The Highway Code
- Obey the rules set out in it

Other motoring matters

You must also show knowledge of other motoring matters, including

- Matters not covered in The Highway Code, such as
    - tyre wear
    - car and road safety
    - basic car maintenance
- Behaviour and road holding of vehicles in bad weather

You must show that you know and understand The Highway Code and that you can apply it.

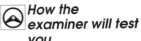 How the examiner will test you

At the end of the test, your examiner will ask you some questions on The Highway Code and on other motoring matters.

You must answer these correctly, although small errors may not cause you to fail.

You will also be asked to identify some traffic signs.

But remember!

Knowing is not enough.

You must demonstrate your knowledge and understanding as you drive.

⊕ What the examiner wants to see

Before you start your engine, you must always check that

- All doors are properly closed
- Your seat and head restraint are correctly adjusted and comfortable
- Your driving mirrors are correctly adjusted
- Your seat belt is fastened, correctly adjusted and comfortable
- The handbrake is on
- The gear lever is in neutral

So develop good habits and practise while you're learning.

Note: If you are driving a car with automatic transmission, you should make the safety checks which apply to your vehicle.

You are advised to study the advice given on driving 'automatics' in the DSA's book, *The Driving Manual* (HMSO).

✗ Faults you must avoid

When the car is moving, never

- Adjust your seat. This is extremely dangerous.
- Adjust your seat belt
- Adjust any of your driving mirrors
- Hold on to the handbrake or gear lever unnecessarily

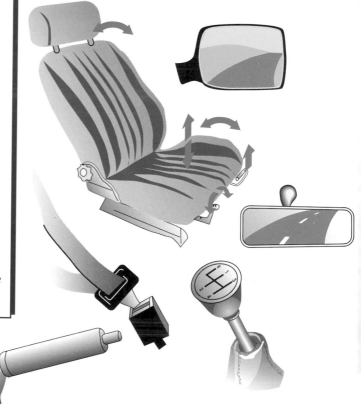

What the test requires

You must show the examiner that you under-stand the functions of all the controls and can use them

- Smoothly
- Correctly
- Safely
- At the right time

The main controls are

- Accelerator
- Clutch
- Footbrake
- Handbrake
- Steering
- Gears

You must

- Understand what these controls do
- Be able to use them competently

How the examiner will test you

For this aspect of driving, there is no special exercise.

The examiner will watch you carefully to see how you use these controls.

Note: If your vehicle has automatic transmission, study the details which apply to you.

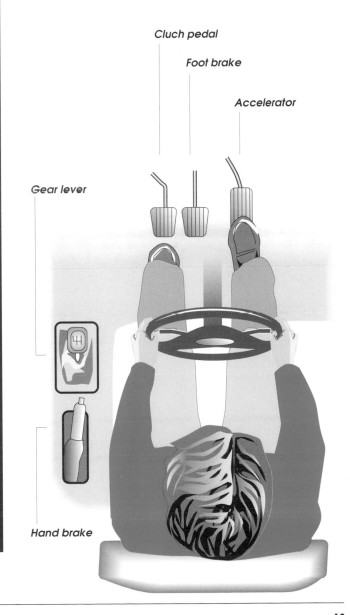

Cluch pedal

Foot brake

Accelerator

Gear lever

Hand brake

The car controls — accelerator, clutch, gears, and brakes

Skills you must master

Accelerator and clutch

- Balance accelerator and clutch to pull away smoothly
- Accelerate evenly to gain speed
- When stopping the car, press the clutch in just before the car stops

Gears

- Choose the right gear for your speed and the road conditions
- Change gear in good time before a hazard or junction

Footbrake

- Brake in good time
- Brake lightly in most situations

Handbrake

- Know how and when to apply the handbrake

✗ Faults you must avoid

Accelerator

- Accelerating fiercely, especially making the tyres screech — distracting or alarming other road users

Clutch

- Jerky and uncontrolled use of the clutch when moving off or changing gear

Gears

- Taking your eyes off the road when you change gear
- Coasting with
  - clutch pedal pressed in, or
  - gear lever in neutral
- Holding on to the gear lever unnecessarily

Footbrake

- Braking harshly, except in emergency

Handbrake

- Never apply the handbrake before the car has stopped
- Never move off with the handbrake on

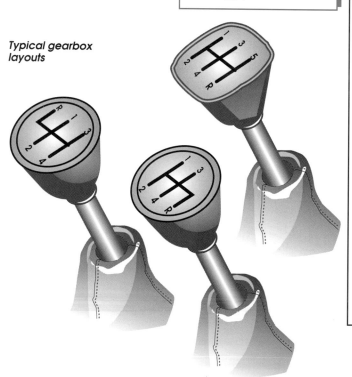

Typical gearbox layouts

✓ Skills you must master

Steering

- Place your hands on the steering wheel in either the 'ten-to-two' or 'quarter-to-three' position, whichever is most comfortable
- Keep your steering movements steady and smooth
- When turning a corner, begin turning the steering wheel at the correct time

✗ Faults you must avoid

Steering

- Never turn too early when steering around a corner. If you do, you risk

    - cutting the corner when turning right and putting other road users at risk

    - striking the kerb when turning left

- Never turn too late. You could put other road users at risk by

    - swinging wide at left turns

    - overshooting right turns

- Crossing your hands on the steering wheel
- Never allow the wheel to spin back after turning
- Resting your arm on the door

Correct hand positions for steering

You must understand

- The functions of *all* controls and switches which have a bearing on road safety

For example:
- indicators
- lights
- windscreen wipers
- demisters

- The meaning of gauges or other displays on the instrument panel

For example:
- speedometer
- various warning lights

 Safety checks

You should also be able to

- Carry out routine safety checks such as
  - oil and coolant levels
  - tyre pressures
- Identify defects especially with
  - steering
  - brakes
  - tyres
  - seat belts
  - lights
  - reflectors
  - horn
  - rear view mirrors
  - speedometer
  - exhaust system
  - direction indicators
  - windscreen wipers and washers
- Understand the effects which
  - a roof rack and luggage
  - extra passengers

will have on the handling of your vehicle.

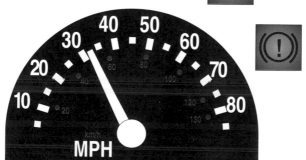

What the test requires

You must be able to move off

- Safely
- Under control

1. On the flat
2. From behind a parked car
3. On a hill, where appropriate

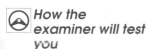
How the examiner will test you

The examiner will watch your use of the controls each time you move off.

✓ Skills you must show

1. Use your mirrors. Signal if necessary
2. Before you move off, look around for
   - Traffic
   - Pedestrians outside the range of your mirrors
3. Move off under control making balanced and safe use of
   - Accelerator
   - Clutch
   - Brakes
   - Steering
4. Use the correct gear

✗ Faults you must avoid

- Pulling out without looking
- Causing other road users to stop or alter their course
- Excessive acceleration
- Moving off in too high a gear
- Failing to co-ordinate the controls correctly and stalling the engine

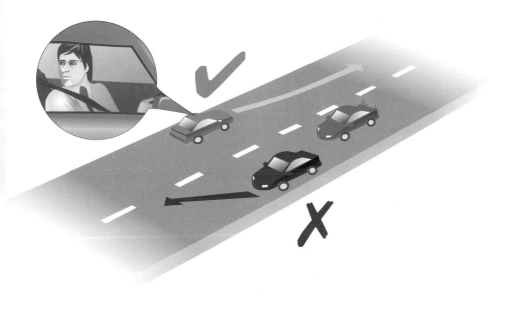

The emergency stop

 What the test requires

In an emergency you must be able to stop the car

- As quickly as possible
- Safely under control
- Without locking the wheels

 How the examiner will test you

The examiner will

1. Ask you to pull up at the side of the road
2. Ask you to make an emergency stop when you are given a signal
3. Demonstrate the signal to you

When the examiner gives the signal, try to stop the car as you would in a real emergency.

- You must react quickly
- Try to stop in a straight line
- Take special care if the road is wet

The examiner might not ask you to do this exercise if you have to make a real emergency stop during the test.

 Skills you must show

Stopping the car

- In the shortest safe distance
- Under full control
- Without risk to other road users

 Faults you must avoid

- Skidding out of control
- Allowing the car to swing off course

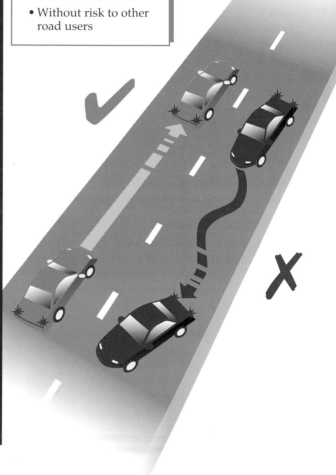

What the test requires

You must be able to reverse your car

- Smoothly
- Correctly
- Safely
- Under full control

 Skills you must master

- Reversing under full control
- Keeping reasonably close to the kerb, without striking or mounting it

 Faults you must avoid

- Mounting the kerb
- Swinging out wide
- Keeping too far from the kerb
- Not showing consideration or causing danger to other road users

 How the examiner will test you

The examiner will

- Ask you to pull up just before a side road on the left
- Point out the side road and ask you to reverse into it

When the examiner asks you

- Make sure you can carry out the exercise correctly and safely
- Check traffic and road conditions in all directions
- Reverse around the corner, keeping a good lookout for traffic or pedestrians
- Straighten up your car and continue to reverse for a reasonable distance
- Pull up in a safe position and wait for the examiner's next instruction

Your seat belt

You may undo your seat belt for the whole exercise.

Do so only if it interferes with your driving, and don't forget to re-fasten it before you move forward after the exercise.

Note: If the view to the rear is restricted (in a van, for example) the examiner might ask you to reverse into a road on the right.

Remember!

Your car will swing out at the front as you reverse around the corner, so keep a good lookout for other road users.

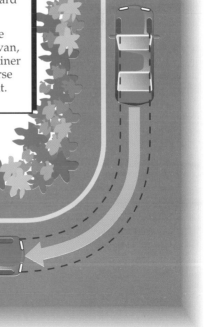

Reverse parking

What the test requires

You must be able to park your car safely at the kerb by reversing into the space of about two car lengths.

How the examiner will test you

When the examiner points out a parked car and asks you to reverse park behind it

- Drive alongside the parked car and position your car so that you can carry out the exercise correctly and safely

Note: Select reverse gear – your reversing lights might help other road users to understand your intention

Take all round observation

- Reverse into the space behind the parked car, *within* the space of about two car lengths
- Stop reasonably close to the kerb

✓ Skills you must master

Safe, steady and controlled parking.

✗ Faults you must avoid

- Getting too close to the parked car
- Mounting the kerb
- Swinging your car from side to side
- Parking too far from the kerb
- Not showing consideration, or causing danger to other road users

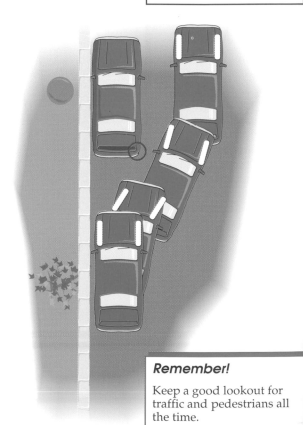

Remember!

Keep a good lookout for traffic and pedestrians all the time.

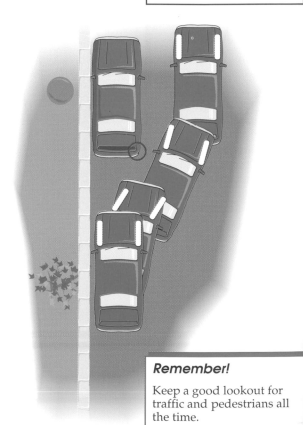

Driving Standards Agency

What the test requires

You must be able to turn your car around in the road

- So it faces in the opposite direction
- Using forward and reverse gears

This will take at least three moves, but make as few as you can.

 ## How the examiner will test you

The examiner will

- Indicate a suitable place and ask you to pull up
- Ask you to turn around in the road.
- Before you begin, make sure the road is clear in both directions
- Drive forward in first gear and turn the steering wheel to the right as much as possible
- Steer briskly to the left just before you pull up close to the opposite kerb
- Check all round, especially your blind spots
- Reverse, turning your steering wheel to the left as much as possible

- Steer briskly to the right just before you pull up close to the kerb behind you
- Repeat if necessary until your car is facing the opposite direction

✗ Faults you must avoid

- Mounting the kerb. (Try not to touch it)
- Not showing consideration or causing danger to other road users

 ## ✓ Skills you must master

You must

- Control your car smoothly
- Make proper use of the
  - accelerator
  - clutch
  - brakes
  - steering
- Show awareness of other road users. All-round observation is essential throughout the manoeuvre.

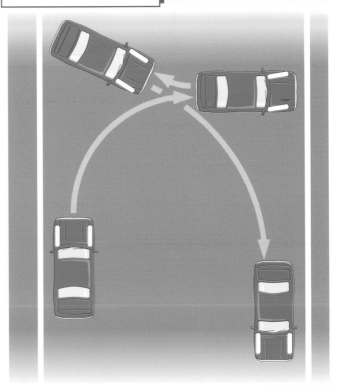

What the test requires

Make sure you use your mirrors effectively

- Before any manoeuvre
- To keep up to date on what is happening behind you

Check carefully before

- Moving off
- Signalling
- Changing direction
- Turning left or right
- Overtaking or changing lane
- Increasing speed
- Slowing down or stopping
- Opening your car door

 How the examiner will test you

For this aspect of driving, there is no special test.

The examiner will watch your use of mirrors as you drive.

 Skills you must show

- Using the Mirrors-Signal-Manoeuvre (MSM) routine (see page 27). Practise
  - looking before you signal
  - looking and signalling before you act
- Acting sensibly and safely on what you see in the mirrors
- Being aware that the mirrors will not show everything behind you

✗ Faults you must avoid

- Manoeuvring without looking in the mirrors
- Not acting on what you see when you look in the mirrors

Just looking is not enough!

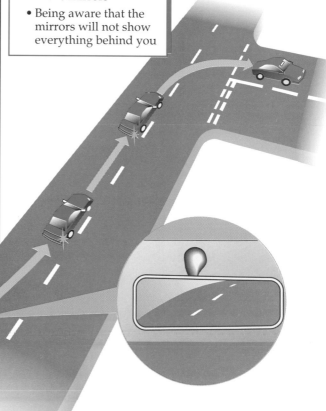

What the test requires

You must signal
- To let others know what you intend to do
- To help other road users, including pedestrians
- In plenty of time

You must only use the signals shown in The Highway Code.

Your signals must help other road users
- To understand what you intend to do
- To react safely

Always make sure your signal is cancelled after use.

How the examiner will test you

For this aspect of driving, there is no special exercise.

The examiner will watch carefully how you use your signals as you drive.

Skills you must master

Giving signals
- Clearly
- In good time

You should also know how to give arm signals and when they are necessary.

Faults you must avoid

- Giving signals carelessly
- Misleading other road users
- Forgetting to cancel the signal
- Waving pedestrians to cross the road

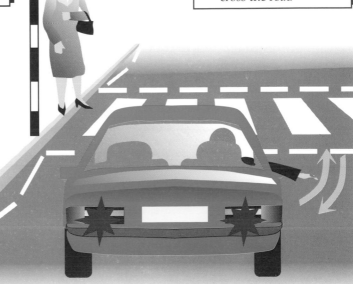

Acting on signs and signals

What the test requires

You must
- Be able to understand
  - all traffic signs
  - road markings
- React to them safely and in good time

At the beginning of the test, the examiner will ask you to follow the road ahead.

Do so unless traffic signs tell you otherwise or you are asked to turn.

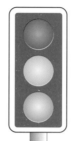

GIVE WAY
50 yds

30

Traffic lights

You must
- Act correctly at traffic lights
- When the green light shows, check that the road is clear before proceeding

Signals by authorised persons

You must obey the signals given by
- police officers
- traffic wardens
- school crossing patrols

Traffic Calming measures

Take extra care on roads which have been altered by the addition of
- 20mph speed limit zone signs
- Speed reduction humps
- Reduced road width marked by bollards, posts or paved areas

What the test requires

You must

- Make reasonable progress along the road
- Drive at a speed appropriate to road and traffic conditions
- Move off at junctions as soon as it is safe to do so

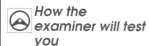 **How the examiner will test you**

For this aspect of driving, there is no special exercise.

The examiner will watch your driving, and will want to see you

- Making reasonable progress along the road
- Keeping up with traffic
- Showing confidence and sound judgement

 Skills you must master

You must be able to

- Choose the correct speed for
  - the type of road
  - the type and density of traffic
  - the weather and visibility
- Approach all hazards at a safe speed without
  - being too cautious
  - interfering with the progress of other traffic

 Faults you must avoid

You must not

- Drive too slowly. You could hold up traffic
- Be overcautious and stop or wait when it's safe and normal to proceed

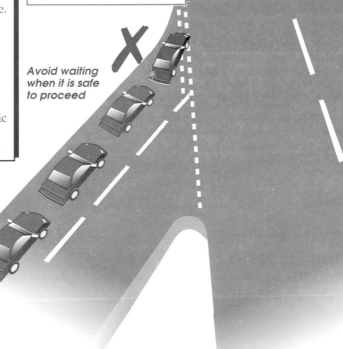

Avoid waiting when it is safe to proceed

Controlling your speed

 What the test requires

You must make good progress along the road, bearing in mind

- Road conditions
- Traffic
- Weather
- Road signs and speed limits

 How the examiner will test you

For this aspect of driving, there is no special exercise.

The examiner will watch carefully your control of speed as you drive.

 Skills you must master

You must

- Take great care in the use of speed
- Make sure you can stop safely, well within the distance you can see to be clear
- Leave a safe distance between yourself and other vehicles
- Leave extra distance on wet or slippery roads
- Drive at a steady speed within the speed limit

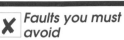 **Faults you must avoid**

- Driving too fast for the road or traffic conditions
- Changing your speed erratically

Select a speed to suit road and traffic conditions

What is a hazard?

A hazard is any situation which could involve adjusting speed or altering course.

Look well ahead where there are

- Road junctions or roundabouts
- Parked vehicles
- Cyclists or horse riders
- Pedestrian crossings

By identifying the hazard early, you will have time to take the appropriate action.

What the test requires

Approaching a hazard

Mirrors-Signal-Manoeuvre (MSM routine)

Always use this routine when approaching a hazard.

M - Mirrors

Check the position of traffic behind you.

S - Signal

Signal your intention to change course or slow down. Signal in good time.

M - Manoeuvre

A manoeuvre is any change of speed or position, from slowing or stopping the car to turning off a busy main road.

What the test requires

You should

- Use the MSM routine when you approach a junction or roundabout

- Position your car correctly. Adjust your speed. Stop if necessary

- If the road has lane markings, use the correct lane. In a one-way street, choose that lane as soon as you can

- If the road has no lane markings

    - when turning left, keep to the left, and watch out for

      motorcyclists and cyclists coming up on your left

      pedestrians crossing

    - when turning right, keep as close to the centre of the road as is safe

- Make sure you take effective observation before you enter a junction

 How the examiner will test you

For this aspect of driving, there is no special exercise.

The examiner will watch carefully and take account of your

- Use of the MSM routine

- Position and speed of approach

- Observation and judgement

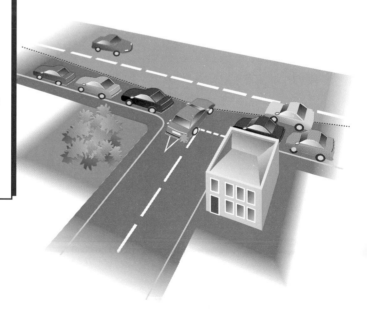

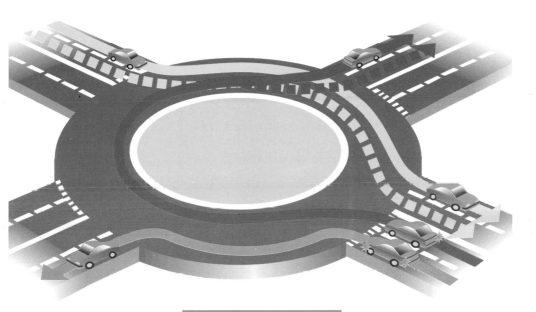

✓ Skills you must master

You must be able to

- Read the road signs and markings accurately (stop signs, give way signs, and so on)
- Judge the correct approach speed
- Slow down in good time and without braking hard
- Judge the speed of traffic, especially at roundabouts and when joining major roads

✗ Faults you must avoid

- Approaching the junction at the wrong speed
- Positioning and turning incorrectly
- Stopping or waiting unnecessarily
- Entering a junction unsafely

What the test requires

When overtaking you must

- Allow enough room
- Give motorcyclists, cyclists and horse riders at least as much room as a car. They can swerve or wobble suddenly
- Allow enough space after overtaking. Don't cut in

Do not overtake

- If the road is too narrow
- When your view is too limited
- Where signs or road markings prohibit overtaking

How the examiner will test you

For this aspect of driving, there is no special exercise.

The examiner will watch carefully and take account of your

- Use of the MSM routine
- Reactions to road and traffic conditions
- Handling of the controls

Skills you must master

You must be able to

- Take stock of the speed and position of vehicles
  - just behind which may be trying to overtake you
  - just in front of any vehicles you are planning to overtake
  - coming towards you
- Overtake only when you can do so
  - safely
  - without causing other vehicles to slow down or alter course

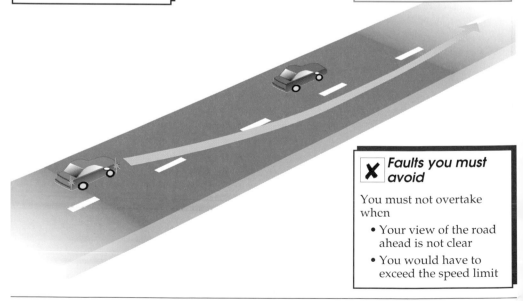

✗ Faults you must avoid

You must not overtake when

- Your view of the road ahead is not clear
- You would have to exceed the speed limit

What the test requires

You must be able to meet and deal with oncoming traffic safely and confidently.

This mainly applies

- On narrow roads, or
- Where there are parked cars or other obstructions
- If there is an obstruction on your side of the road, or not enough room for two vehicles to pass safely
  - use the MSM routine
  - slow down and be prepared to stop
- When you need to stop, keep well back from the obstruction to give yourself
  - a better view of the road ahead
  - room to move off easily when the way is clear
- If possible when you are passing parked cars, allow at least the width of a car door

How the examiner will test you

For this aspect of driving, there is no special exercise.

The examiner will watch carefully and take account of your

- Use of the MSM routine
- Reactions to road and traffic conditions.
- Handling of the controls

✓ Skills you must master

You must

- Show judgement when meeting oncoming traffic
- Be decisive when stopping and moving off
- Allow enough room when passing parked cars

Watch out for

- Doors opening
- Children running out
- Pedestrians stepping out
- Vehicles pulling out without warning

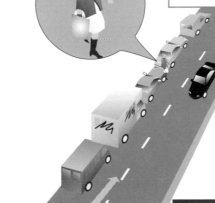

✘ Faults you must avoid

Causing other vehicles to
- Slow down
- Swerve
- Stop

What the test requires

You must be able to cross the path of other vehicles safely and with confidence.

Crossing the path of other vehicles occurs mainly when you have to turn right into a side road or driveway.

You should

- Use the MSM routine
- Position your car correctly. Adjust your speed
- Keep as close to the centre of the road as is safe.
- Watch out for approaching traffic. Stop if necessary.
- Watch out for pedestrians
  - crossing at the side road
  - on the pavement, if you are entering a driveway

How the examiner will test you

For this aspect of driving, there is no special exercise.

The examiner will watch carefully and take account of your judgement of oncoming traffic.

Skills you must master

You must show sound judgement before turning across the path of oncoming traffic

Faults you must avoid

- Causing other vehicles to
  - slow down
  - swerve
  - stop
- Cutting the corner

And you should not

- Go beyond the correct turning point before you begin to turn

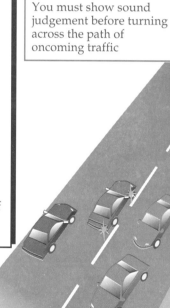

What the test requires

You must always drive at such a speed that you can stop in the distance you can see to be clear.

Always keep a safe separation distance between you and the vehicle in front.

In good conditions, leave a gap of at least one metre (or yard) for each MPH of your speed – or a two-second time gap.

In bad conditions leave at least double the distance or a four-second time gap.

In slow-moving congested traffic it may not be practical to leave as much space.

 How the examiner will test you

For this aspect of driving, there is no special exercise.

The examiner will watch carefully and take account of your
- Use of the MSM routine
- Anticipation
- Reaction to changing road and traffic conditions
- Handling of the controls

 Skills you must master

You must
- Be able to judge a safe separation distance between you and the vehicle ahead
- Show correct use of the MSM routine – especially before reducing speed
- Avoid the need to brake sharply if the vehicle in front slows down or stops
- Take extra care when your view ahead is limited by large vehicles such as lorries or buses

Watch out for
- Brake lights ahead
- Direction indicators
- Vehicles ahead braking without warning

 Faults you must avoid
- Following too closely
- Braking suddenly
- Swerving to avoid the vehicle in front slowing down or stopping

What the test requires

You should

- Normally keep well to the left
- Keep clear of parked vehicles
- Avoid weaving in and out between parked vehicles
- Position your vehicle correctly for the direction you intend to take
- Obey lane markings – especially
  - Left/right turn arrows at junctions
  - When approaching roundabouts
  - In one-way streets
  - Bus lanes

How the examiner will test you

For this aspect of driving, there is no special exercise.

The examiner will watch carefully to see that you

- Use the MSM routine
- Select the correct lane in good time

Skills you must master

You must

- Plan ahead and choose the correct lane in good time
- Use the MSM routine correctly
- Position your vehicle sensibly – even if there are no lane markings shown

Faults you must avoid

- Driving too close to the kerb
- Driving too close to the centre of the road
- Changing lanes at the last moment or without good reason
- Hindering other road users by being badly positioned or in the wrong lane
- Straddling lanes or lane markings
- Cutting across the path of other road users in another lane at roundabouts

What the test requires

You must

- Recognise the different types of pedestrian crossing
- Show courtesy and consideration towards pedestrians
- Stop safely when necessary

At all pedestrian crossings

You must slow down and stop if there is anyone on the crossing.

At zebra crossings

You should

- Slow down and be prepared to stop if there is anyone waiting to cross
- Know the correct arm signal to use before slowing down

At pelican, puffin and toucan crossings

You must

- Stop if the lights are red
- Stop at the amber lights if you can do so safely
- Give way to any pedestrians on a pelican crossing when the amber lights are flashing
- Give way to cyclists on a toucan crossing as you would to pedestrians

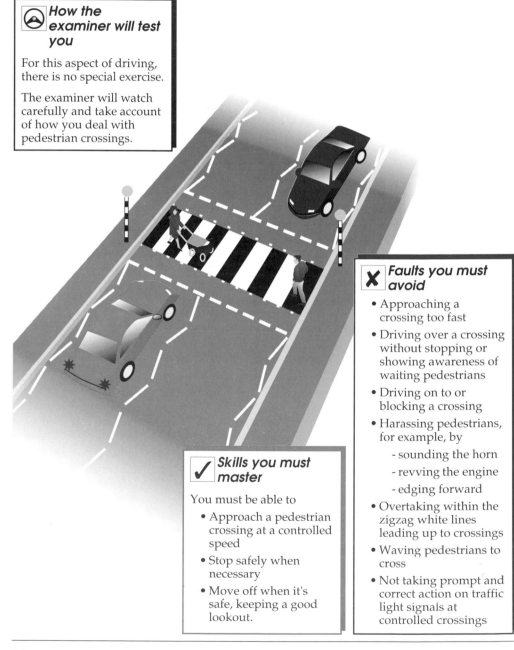

🔄 How the examiner will test you

For this aspect of driving, there is no special exercise.

The examiner will watch carefully and take account of how you deal with pedestrian crossings.

✗ Faults you must avoid

- Approaching a crossing too fast
- Driving over a crossing without stopping or showing awareness of waiting pedestrians
- Driving on to or blocking a crossing
- Harassing pedestrians, for example, by
  - sounding the horn
  - revving the engine
  - edging forward
- Overtaking within the zigzag white lines leading up to crossings
- Waving pedestrians to cross
- Not taking prompt and correct action on traffic light signals at controlled crossings

✓ Skills you must master

You must be able to

- Approach a pedestrian crossing at a controlled speed
- Stop safely when necessary
- Move off when it's safe, keeping a good lookout.

What the test requires

When you make a normal stop, you must be able to

- Select a place where you will not
  - obstruct the road
  - create a hazard
- Stop close to the edge of the road

How the examiner will test you

For this aspect of driving, there is no special exercise.

The examiner will watch your driving and take account of your

- Use of the MSM routine
- Judgement in selecting a safe place to stop

Skills you must master

You must know

- How and where to stop without causing inconvenience or danger to other road users

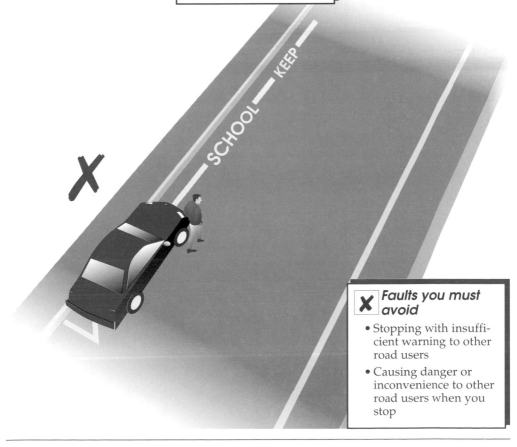

X Faults you must avoid

- Stopping with insufficient warning to other road users
- Causing danger or inconvenience to other road users when you stop

What the test requires

■ Awareness

You must be aware of other road users at all times

■ Anticipation

You should always plan ahead

- Judge what other road users are going to do
- Predict how their actions would affect you
- React safely and in good time

 ## What the examiner wants to see

You must show

- Awareness of and consideration for all road users, and
- Anticipation of possible danger and concern for safety

For example

■ Pedestrians

- Give way to pedestrians when turning from one road into another
- Take particular care with the very young, the disabled, and the elderly. They may not have seen you and could step out suddenly

■ Cyclists

Take special care

- When crossing bus or cycle lanes
- With riders passing on your left
- With children cycling

■ Moped riders or Motorcyclists

Look out for mopeds or motorcycles

- In slow-moving traffic
- Coming up on your left
- At junctions

■ Animals

Take special care with people in charge of animals, especially horse riders

X Faults you must avoid

- Reacting suddenly to road or traffic conditions rather than anticipating them
- Showing irritation with other road users, particularly cyclists or pedestrians
- Sounding your horn aggressively
- Revving your engine or edging forward when waiting for pedestrians to cross.

Motorcycle Riders

To ride a motorcycle on the public road, you must

- Be at least 17 years of age
- Have a driving licence which specifies you are entitled to ride motorcycles (Category A - formerly Group D)

That licence can be any of the following

1. Full Motorcycle Licence
2. Provisional Motorcycle Licence*
3. Full Car or Moped Licence. These automatically give provisional motorcycle entitlement*
4. A Provisional Driving Licence with provisional motorcycle entitlement*

* If you hold one of these licences, see Compulsory Basic Training and Provisional Motorcycle Entitlement on this page.

Compulsory Basic Training (CBT)

Before you are allowed to ride on the road unsupervised, you must attend a CBT course, if

- The provisional motorcycle entitlement of your licence started on or after 1st December 1990, and
- You do not hold a valid Part 1 Test Certificate

When you have reached a satisfactory standard, you will be issued with a Certificate of Completion (DL 196).

You are allowed to ride on the road without taking a CBT course, if

- You hold a licence with provisional motorcycle entitlement which started before 1st December 1990
- You hold a valid Part 1 Test Certificate

However, you must have a DL 196 certificate or a valid Part 1 Test Certificate before you can take the Motorcycle test.

Provisional Motorcycle Entitlement

This entitles learners to ride a machine of up to 125cc or a maximum power output of 9kW.

You must not

- Ride on motorways
- Carry a pillion passenger
- Ride without L-plates

Two-year limit

A Provisional Motorcycle Licence is valid for two years only. You must take and pass the Motorcycle Test within two years, or you'll have to wait a year before you can apply for another provisional licence.

This restriction does not apply if your provisional motorcycle entitlement from age 17 is granted by a full car or moped licence.

Element 1: Introduction

Before you do any practical training you must be told and understand

- The aims of the compulsory basic training course
- The importance of the right equipment and clothing
- The need to be clearly visible to other road users
- Legal requirements when riding on the road
- Why motorcyclists are more vulnerable than other road users
- The need to drive at correct speeds, according to road and traffic conditions
- The importance of reading and understanding The Highway Code

Your eyesight

You must be able to read in good daylight a number-plate

- Containing letters and figures 79.4 mm (3.1 inches) high
- At a distance of 20.5 metres (67 feet)
- With the aid of glasses or contact lenses if you normally wear them

Element 2: Practical on-site training

You must become familiar with the motorcycle, its controls and how it works, and be able to

- Carry out basic machine checks, and be able to take the bike on and off the stand

- Wheel your motorcycle around to the left and right showing proper balance, and stop the motorcycle by braking

- Stop and start the engine satisfactorily

Compulsory training for motorcycle learners

 **Element 3:
Practical on-site
riding**

You must be able to

- Ride your motorcycle
  under control in a
  straight line, and bring
  it to a controlled stop
- Carry out controlled
  braking using both
  brakes
- Change gear
  satisfactorily
- Carry out rear
  observation correctly

- Carry out simulated
  left and right turns
  correctly using the
  routines
    - Observation-
      Signal-Manoeuvre
      (OSM)
    - Position-Speed-
      Look (PSL)
- Ride your motorcycle
  in a figure of eight
  circuit under control
- Ride your motorcycle
  slowly under control
- Bring your motorcycle
  to a stop under full
  control in an
  emergency

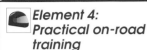

Element 4: Practical on-road training

You must understand the need to, and be able to

- Ride defensively and anticipate the actions of other road users
- Use rear observation at appropriate times
- Assume the correct road position when riding
- Leave sufficient space when following another vehicle
- Pay due regard to the effect of varying weather when riding
- Be aware of the various types of road surfaces you can meet

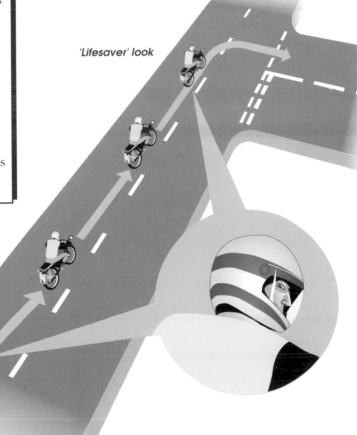

'Lifesaver' look

Look before you signal

Element 5: Practical on-road riding

You must be able to ride safely under a variety of road and traffic conditions including as many of these as possible

- Roundabouts
- Junctions
- Pedestrian crossings
- Traffic lights
- Gradients
- Bends and obstructions

The Certificate of Completion (DL196)

When you have successfully completed the course you will be given a Certificate of Completion of an Approved Training Course.

You must either

- Send this with your application form when applying for the motorcycle test, or
- Present it when you attend for your test

Note: Your test will be cancelled if you fail to do so.

The Approved Training Body will also wish to talk to you about the need for further training to prepare you for your test.

DRIVING STANDARDS AGENCY

000000

Road Traffic Act 1988

Certificate of Completion of an Approved Training Course for Motor Vehicles in Categories A and P

Driver Number of Candidate

Date and time of course completion | Hrs | Mins

Current name

Current address

Postcode

has successfully completed an approved training course for motor vehicles in categories A and P, prescribed for the purpose of Section 97 of the Road Traffic Act 1988 as amended by Section 6 of the Road Traffic (Driver Licensing and Information Systems) Act 1989.

Signature of Instructor — appointed to conduct such training

Initials and Surname (BLOCK CAPITALS) — No.

The successful candidate should sign in ink below in the presence of the instructor.

Signature

Official Stamp of Training Body | Site at which Course conducted and Site No.

Please read the notes overleaf — DL 196

An Executive Agency of the Department of Transport

Fig. 6.4 Certificate of completion (DL196)

Special features

The driving test also applies to motorcycles. You should study Section 1 and the parts of Section 2 which apply to the motorcycle test.

The following are some extra requirements

Braking

You must be able combine the use of front and rear brakes correctly, in all weather conditions.

Make sure your instructor explains fully and you understand the correct braking techniques and their use.

Emergency Stop

- Apply the front brake just before the rear
- Apply both brakes effectively
- Stop the machine as quickly as possible without locking either wheel

Turn in road

After the emergency stop exercise the examiner will ask you to ride in a U-turn and stop on the other side of the road.

Slow Ride

You may be asked to ride as in slow-moving traffic for a short distance, if the examiner has not already seen you doing this in normal traffic.

Rear Observation

Even if you have mirrors fitted to your motorcycle, look over the appropriate shoulder to check the position of traffic before you

- Signal
- Change direction
- Slow down or stop

Take note of what you see and act on it.

Just looking is not enough!

How the examiner will test you

When you are taking the test, the examiner will follow you either on a motorcycle or in a car, except during the emergency stop exercise.

Your test will be carried out over a route covering a wide variety of traffic conditions.

Before the test you will be fitted with

- Earphones under your helmet
- A radio receiver on a waist belt

Section 4
Officially recommended syllabus for learning to drive

Driving is a life skill. It will take you many years to fully master the skills set out here.

The syllabus lists the skills in which you must achieve basic competence in order to pass the Driving Test.

You must also have
- a thorough knowledge of The Highway Code and the motoring laws
- a thorough understanding of your responsibilities as a driver

This means that you must have real concern, not just for your own safety, but for the safety of all road users, including pedestrians.

Make sure your instructor covers the syllabus fully.

1. Legal requirements

To learn to drive you must

i. be at least 17 years old. If you receive a mobility allowance for a disability you may start driving a car at 16.

ii. be able to read in good daylight, with glasses or contact lenses if you wear them, a motor vehicle number-plate
- 20.5m (approx. 67ft) away
- with letters 79.4mm (3.1 inches) high

iii. be medically fit to drive

iv. hold a provisional licence or comply with the conditions for holding a provisional licence (see leaflet D100*)

v. ensure that the vehicle being driven
- is legally roadworthy
- has a current test certificate, if over the prescribed age
- displays a valid tax disc

vi. make sure that the vehicle being driven is properly insured for its use

vii. display L-plates which are visible from the front and the back of the vehicle

viii. be supervised by a person who
- has held (and still holds) a full licence for the category of vehicle being driven for at least three years
- is at least 21 years old

ix. wear a seat belt, unless granted an exemption, and see that all the seat belts in the vehicle and their anchorages and fittings are free from obvious defects

x. ensure that children under 14 are suitably restrained by the appropriate child restraint or an adult seat belt

xi. be aware of the legal requirement to notify medical conditions which could affect safe driving. If a vehicle has been adapted for disability, ensure that the adaptations are suitable to control the vehicle safely.

xii. know the rules on the issue, presentation or display of
- driving licences
- insurance certificates
- tax discs

2. Car controls, equipment and components

You must

i. understand the function of the
- accelerator
- clutch
- gears
- footbrake
- handbrake
- steering

and be able to use these competently

ii. know the function of other controls and switches in the car that have a bearing on road safety and use them competently

iii. understand the meaning of the gauges and other displays on the instrument panel

iv. know the legal requirements for the vehicle

v. be able to carry out routine safety checks such as
- oil and coolant levels
- tyre pressures

and identify defects especially with
- steering
- brakes
- tyres
- seat belts
- lights
- reflectors
- direction indicators
- windscreen wipers and washers
- horn
- rear view mirrors
- speedometer
- exhaust system

vi. understand the effects which a loaded roof rack or extra passengers will have on the handling of your vehicle

3. Road user behaviour

You must

i. know the most common causes of accidents

ii. know which road users are most at risk and how to reduce that risk

iii. know the rules, risks and effects of drinking and driving

iv. know the effect of fatigue, illness and drugs on driving performance

v. be aware of age dependent problems among other road users especially among children, teenagers and the elderly

*Leaflet D100 contains general information on driver licensing and is free from DVLC Swansea or any Post Office.

i. be alert and be able to anticipate the likely actions of other road users and be able to suggest appropriate precautions

ii. be aware that courtesy and consideration towards road users are essential for safe driving

4. Vehicle characteristics

You must

i. know the most important principles concerning braking distances and road holding under various road and weather conditions

ii. know the handling characteristics of other vehicles with regard to stability, speed, braking and manoeuvrability

iii. know that some vehicles are less easily seen than others

iv. be able to assess the risks caused by the characteristics of other vehicles and suggest precautions that can be taken, for example

- large commercial vehicles pulling to the right before turning left
- blind spots for drivers of some commercial vehicles
- bicycles and motorcycles being buffeted by strong wind

5. Road and weather conditions

You must

i. know the particular hazards of driving

- in both daylight and dark
- on different types of road, for example
  - on single carriageways, including country lanes
  - on three-lane roads
  - on dual-carriageways and motorways

ii. gain experience in driving on urban and higher speed roads (but not motorways) in both daylight and darkness

iii. know which road surfaces provide the better or poorer grip when braking

iv. know the hazards caused by bad weather, for example
- rain   - fog
- snow   - icy roads
- strong cross winds

v. be able to assess the risks caused by road and traffic conditions, be aware of how the conditions may cause others to drive unsafely, and be able to take appropriate precautions

6. Traffic signs, rules and regulations

You must

i. have a sound knowledge of the meaning of traffic signs and road markings

ii. have a sound grasp of the traffic signs, for example
- speed limits
- parking restrictions
- zebra and pelican crossings

7. Car control and road procedure

You must have the knowledge and skill to carry out the following tasks safely and competently
- making proper use of mirrors, observation, and signals

i. take necessary precautions before getting into or out of the vehicle

ii. before starting the engine
- carry out safety checks including
  - doors
  - seat and head restraint
  - seatbelt
  - mirrors
- take proper precautions
- check that the handbrake is on and the gear lever in neutral

iii. start the engine and move off
- straight ahead and at an angle
- on the level, uphill and downhill

iv. select the correct road position for normal driving

v. take proper observation in all traffic conditions

vi. drive at a speed suitable for road and traffic conditions

vii. react promptly to all risks

viii. change traffic lanes

ix. pass stationary vehicles

x. meet, overtake and cross the path of other vehicles

xi. turn right and left, and at junctions, including crossroads and roundabouts

xii. drive ahead at crossroads and roundabouts

xiii. keep a safe separation gap when following other vehicles

xiv. act correctly at pedestrian crossings

xv. show proper regard for the safety of other road users, with particular care towards the most vulnerable

xvi. drive on both urban and rural roads and, where possible, dual carriageways — keeping up with the traffic flow where it is safe and proper to do so

Officially recommended syllabus for learning to drive

xvii. comply with traffic regulations and traffic signs and signals given by the police, traffic wardens and other road users

xviii. stop the vehicle safely, normally and in an emergency, without locking the wheels

xix. turn the vehicle in the road to face the opposite way using forward and reverse gears

xx. reverse the vehicle into a side road keeping reasonably close to the kerb

xxi. park parallel to the kerb while driving in reverse gear

xxii. park the vehicle in a multistorey car park, or other parking bay, on the level, uphill and downhill, both in forward and reverse direction

xxiii. cross all types of railway level crossings

8. Additional knowledge

You must know

i. the importance of correct tyre pressures

ii. the action to avoid and correct skids

iii. how to drive through floods and flooded areas

iv. what to do if involved in an accident or breakdown including the special arrangements for accident and breakdown on motorways

v. basic first aid for use on the road as set out in The Highway Code

vi. the action to take to deter car thieves

9. Motorway driving

You must gain a sound knowledge of the special rules, regulations and driving techniques for motorway driving before taking your driving test.

After passing your test further lessons are recommended with an ADI before driving unsupervised on motorways.

10. Points for riders of mopeds and motorcycles

You must comply with the requirements of a provisional licence

- Display L-plates to the front and the rear
- Solo motorcycles must not exceed 125cc or 9Kw power output
- Pillion passengers must not be carried
- Riding on motorways is not allowed

You must master everything in Sections 1–9, except the items which clearly do not refer to you.

In addition a learner rider must

i. know the safety factors relating to safety helmets and how to adjust the helmet correctly

ii. know the safety factors in wearing suitable clothing and in using goggles or a visor

iii. know the importance of rear observation
- by use of mirrors
- by looking over the shoulder
- including the life-saver look

iv. know how to lean while turning

v. be able to carry out additional safety checks for two-wheel vehicles, for example
- chain tension and condition
- condition of control cables
- steering-head play
- suspension
- wheels, and tightness of all nuts and bolts

vi. be able to use the front and rear brakes correctly

vii. be able to keep the machine balanced at all speeds

viii. be able to make a U-turn safely

ix. be able to wheel the machine, without the aid of the engine, by walking alongside it

x. be able to park and remove the machine from its stand

he condition of your ehicle

our vehicle must be echanically sound.

any modern vehicles are quipped with a spare heel intended for tempo- ry use at restricted peeds.

our vehicle will not be itable for use on test if ne of these spare wheels is use.

ll equipment required by w must be fitted and orking correctly. The ngine must not be altered run especially fast. This n cause loss of control.

he controls, seating or any quipment or articles in the r must be arranged so ey do not interfere with e conduct of the test.

dual accelerator (if fitted) ust be removed.

our examiner must be able see clearly through the ar window.

eat belts

the law requires your ehicle to have seat belts, ake sure that

- They work properly
- They are in a clean and satisfactory condition

ear your seat belt, unless ou have a medical exemp- n certificate.

Reversing

You are allowed to remove your seat belt when revers- ing your vehicle. Make sure you fasten it immediately afterwards.

Examiner's seat belt

The examiner will normally want to wear a seat belt, although examiners are exempt in some circum- stances.

If the examiner is not able to fasten a seat belt, your test will be cancelled and you will lose your fee.

Left-hand drive vehicles

If you are driving a left- hand drive vehicle, take special care and make full use of your mirrors.

Vehicles not suitable for a car driving test

- Vehicles with no clear view to the rear – other than by use of mirrors
- Vehicles with only a driver's seat
- Vehicles with more than eight passenger seats
- Loaded or partly loaded vehicles
- Vehicles over 7.5 tonnes in weight
- Vehicles towing trailers

Large goods and passenger carrying vehicles

For advice on learning to drive or taking a test on a larger vehicle, refer to the DSA books

- Your Large Goods Vehicle Driving Test (HMSO)
- The Bus and Coach Driving Manual (pub. Feb 1995)

Or contact your nearest DSA Office for information.

For licence information, see leaflet D100 obtainable from Vehicle Registration, DSA Regional, Traffic Area or Post Offices.

Motorcyclists

You must wear a safety helmet at all times when riding, unless you are a member of Sikh religion and wear a turban.

If your helmet has a visor, it must conform to the required BSI standard.

Test not conducted

You will lose your fee if your vehicle is not suitable for the test.

Bribery

It is a criminal offence to attempt to bribe an exam- iner in any way.

Retesting disqualified drivers/riders

The new penalties

Tough penalties now exist for anyone convicted of certain dangerous driving offences.

Now courts

- **Will** impose an extended test on anyone convicted of the new dangerous driving offences

- **Can** impose an extended test on anyone convicted of other offences involving obligatory disqualification

- **Can** also order a normal-length test for other endorsable offences before the disqualified driver can recover a full licence

Applying for a retest

A driver subject to a retest can apply for a provisional licence at the end of the disqualification period.

The normal rules for provisional licence holders apply

- The driver must be supervised by a person who

  - has held a full driving licence for at least three years and still holds one for the category of vehicle being driven

  - is at least 21 years of age

- L-plates must be displayed to the front and rear of the vehicle

- Driving on motorways is not allowed

Moped riders and motorcyclists

A rider subject to a retest can also apply for a provisional licence at the end of the disqualification period.

The normal rules for provisional licence holders apply

- L-plates must be displayed to the front and rear of the machine

- Solo motorcycles must not exceed 125cc or 9Kw power output

- Pillion passengers must not be carried

- Riding on motorways is not allowed*

In addition, riders should check whether they have to take a CBT course before riding unsupervised on the road with their provisional licence.

For further information, contact your nearest DSA Regional Office.

* **Note**: Moped riders with a full driving licence are not permitted to ride on motorways.

onger test

he extended driving test
akes about 70 minutes over
wide variety of roads,
sually including dual
arriage-ways.

he questions

he examiner will ask you
bout 10 questions on The
Highway Code and on
ther motoring matters.

ou will also be asked to
dentify about 12 traffic
gns.

More demanding

The extended test is more
demanding. Make sure you
are ready.

You are advised to take
suitable instruction from an
ADI.

Higher fees

The fee reflects the extra
length of the test.

Section 6
DSA Service Standards for Test Candidates

Service Standards for Test Candidates

The Driving Standards Agency is committed to providing the following standard of service for test candidates

- The national average waiting time for a car test will be no more than 6 weeks

- Test appointments will be available within 10 weeks at any permanent test centre

- The national average waiting time for a motorcycle, lorry or bus test will be no more than 4 weeks

- Unsuccessful candidates will be offered an oral and written explanation of the reasons for their test results by the examiner at the end of their test

- Test appointment notification will be issued within 7 working days of receipt of a correctly completed application form and appropriate fee

- 90% of telephone calls to booking offices will be answered within 1 minute

- Refund of test fees will be issued within 3 weeks of a valid claim with supporting information

- All letters to DSA, including complaints, will be answered within 10 working days

Complaints Guide for test candidates

The Driving Standards Agency aims to give our customers the best possible service.

Please tell us

- When we have done well
- When you are not satisfied

Your comments can help us to improve the service we offer.

If you have any questions about how your test was carried out, please contact the local Supervising Examiner whose address is displayed at your local Driving Test Centre.

If you are dissatisfied with the reply or you wish to comment on other matters, you can write to the Regional Manager (Please see the list of Regional Offices inside the back cover).

If your concern relates to an Approved Driving Instructor, you should write to:

The Registrar of Approved Driving Instructors
Driving Standards Agency
Stanley House
Talbot Street
Nottingham
NG1 5GU

Finally, you can write to

The Chief Executive
Driving Standards Agency
Stanley House
Talbot Street
Nottingham
NG1 5GU

None of this removes your right to take your complaint to

- Your Member of Parliament, who can decide to raise your case personally with the DSA Chief Executive, the Minister, or the Parliamentary Commissioner for Administration (the Ombudsman) whose name and address is on page 56

- A Magistrates' Court (in Scotland, to the Sheriff of your area) if you believe that your test was not carried out according to the regulations

  Before doing this, **you should seek legal advice**.

DSA Compensation Code for test candidates

Compensation Code for test candidates

The DSA will normally refund the test fee, or give a free re-booking in the following cases

- Where the appointments are cancelled by us – for any reason

- Where appointments are cancelled by the candidate, who gives at least **10** clear working days notice for car and motorcycle tests, or **5** clear working days notice for lorry and bus tests

- Where the candidate keeps the test appointment, but the test does not take place, or is not completed for reasons not attributable to him/her – nor to any vehicle provided by him/her for the test

In addition we will normally consider reasonable claims from the candidate for financial loss, or expenditure unavoidably and directly incurred by him/her, as a result of DSA cancelling the test at short notice (other than for reasons of bad weather). For example, we will normally consider a claim for the commercial hire of the vehicle for the test.

Applications should be made to the Regional Office where the test was booked.

This Compensation Code does not affect your existing legal rights

If you pass

If you pass, you will have shown that you can drive safely.

You will be given

- A Pass Certificate (D10, or D10ET in the case of extended driving tests), and

- A copy of the Driving Test Report which will show any minor faults which have been marked during the test*

This is to help you to overcome any minor weaknesses in your driving as you gain experience.

Note: Motorcycle Test candidates will only be given a Pass Certificate (Form D10 or D10ET).

Developing driving standards

You should aim to raise your standard of driving with additional instruction and experience.

The 'Pass Plus' scheme has been devised by the Department of Transport in partnership with the insurance industry to enable you to gain experience safely. Your instructor may have details, or you can contact the DSA Head Office for the names of instructors operating in your area.

You may also wish to contact voluntary organisations such as

- The Guild of Experienced Motorists (GEM)

- The Institute of Advanced Motorists (IAM)

- The Royal Society for the Prevention of Accidents (ROSPA)

Motorway driving

Ask your ADI for lessons in motorway driving.

This is important, because you must get experience in driving on motorways before you drive unsupervised on a busy motorway.

If you fail

Your driving will not have been up to the standard required.

You will have made mistakes which could have caused danger on the road.

Your examiner will

- Give you a Statement of Failure including a copy of the Driving Test Report which will show all the faults marked during the test

- Explain briefly why you have failed

Study the Driving Test Report and refer to the relevant sections in this book.

Show your copy of the Driving Test Report to your ADI, who will help you to correct the faults.

Your ADI should not concentrate on your faults, but will aim to continue to improve all aspects of your driving before you retake the test.

Listen to your ADI's advice, and get as much practice as you can.

You must wait one calendar month before you can be tested on a vehicle of the same category.

Right of Appeal

Although the examiner's decision cannot be changed, if you think your test was not carried out according to the regulations, you have a right to appeal.

- If you live in England or Wales, you have 6 months after the issue of the Statement of Failure in which to appeal (Magistrates' Courts Act 1952 [Ch. 55 part VII, Sectn. 104])

- If you live in Scotland, you have 21 days in which to appeal (Sheriff Court, Scotland Act of Sederunt (Statutory Appeals) 1981)

Section 8
List of DSA offices and other useful addresses

DSA Head Office
Stanley House
Talbot Street
Nottingham NG1 5GU
Tel: (0115) 955 7600

DSA Regional Offices
DSA Scotland
Westgate House
Westgate Road
Newcastle-upon-Tyne NE1 1TW
Tel: (0131) 529 8580
Fee enquiry message Tel: (0131) 529 8592
Credit/Debit Cards Tel: (0131) 529 8590

DSA North Eastern Region
Westgate House
Westgate Road
Newcastle-upon-Tyne NE1 1TW
Tel: (0191) 201 4000
Fee and waiting time recorded messages
Tel: (0191) 201 4100
Credit/Debit Cards Tel: (0191) 201 4108

DSA North Western Region
Portcullis House
Seymour Grove
Stretford
Manchester M16 0NE
Tel: (0161) 872 2333
Fees, waiting times & information on
Saturday tests (recorded message)
Tel: (0161) 848 0361
Credit/Debit Cards Tel: (0161) 877 5421

DSA West Midlands Region
Cumberland House
200 Broad Street
Birmingham B15 1TD
Tel: (0121) 643 2020
Fees and waiting times recorded
messages Tel: (0121) 643 3306
Credit/Debit Cards Tel: (0121) 633 4422

DSA Eastern Region (Nottingham)
Stanley House
56 Talbot Street
Nottingham NG1 5GU
Tel: (0115) 924 2111
Fees and general information message
Tel. (0115) 941 0827
Credit/Debit Cards Tel: (0115) 924 0444

DSA Eastern Region (Cambridge)
Stanley House
56 Talbot Street
Nottingham NG1 5GU
Tel: (01223) 301100
Fees and general information message
Tel: (01223) 532111
Credit/Debit Cards Tel: (01223) 301113

DSA Wales
Caradog House
1-6 St Andrews Place
Cardiff CF1 3PW
Tel: (01222) 225186/7/8 and 373400
Fees, waiting time & cancellation
messages Tel: (01222) 395638
Credit/Debit Cards Tel: (01222) 641041

DSA Western Region
Caradog House
1-6 St Andrews Place
Cardiff CF1 3PW
Tel: (0117) 922 1066
Fees recorded message
Tel: (0117) 929 0602
Credit/Debit Cards Tel: (0117) 975 0075

DSA South Eastern Region
Ivy House
3 Ivy Terrace
Eastbourne BN21 4QT
Tel: (0132) 341 7242
Fees and general information messages
Kent/Sussex Tel: (01323) 647946
Oxon/Hants/Bucks/Berks
Tel: (01323) 647935
Credit/Debit Cards Tel: (01323) 417755

DSA Metropolitan Region
PO Box 2224
Charles House
375 Kensington High Street
London W14 8TY
Tel: (0171) 957 0957
Fees recorded message
Tel: (0171) 606 0484
Credit/Debit Cards Tel: (0171) 602 9000

Other useful addresses
Approved Driving Instructors National Joint Council
The Secretary
41 Edinburgh Road
Cambridge CB4 1QR
Tel: (01223) 359079

Department of Transport Mobility Advice and Vehicle Information Service (MAVIS)
The Transport Research Laboratory
Crowthorne
Berkshire RG11 6AU
Tel: (01344) 770456

Driving Instructors Association
The Secretary
Safety House
Beddington Farm Road
Croydon CRO 4XZ
Tel: (0181) 665 5151

Institute of Advanced Motorists
IAM House
359 Chiswick High Road
London W4 4HS
Tel: (0181) 994 4403

Motor Schools Association of Great Britain Ltd
The General Manager
182A Heaton Moor Road
Stockport
Cheshire SK4 4DU
Tel: (0161) 980 5907

National Association of Approved Driving Instructors
90 Ash Lane
Halebarns
Altrincham
Cheshire WA15 8PB
Tel: (0161) 980 5907

The Royal Society for the Prevention Accidents (ROSPA)
22 Summers Road
Acocks Green
Birmingham B27 7UT
Tel: (0121) 706 8121

The Guild of Experienced Motorists
Station Road
Forest Row
East Sussex RH18 5EN
Tel: (01342) 825676

The Parliamentary Commissoner for Administration (The Ombudsman)
W K Reid CB
Church House
Great Smith Street
London SW1p 3BW
Tel: (0171) 276 2003/3000

Printed in the United Kingdom for HMSO
Dd 301591 C800 11/95 59226